The Gentle Whisper

The Gentle Whisper

SERMONS FOR THE FIRST THIRD OF PENTECOST SEASON
(SUNDAYS IN ORDINARY TIME)

DUANE KELDERMAN

SERIES C FIRST LESSON TEXTS FROM
THE COMMON (CONSENSUS) LECTIONARY

C.S.S. Publishing Company, Inc.
Lima, Ohio

THE GENTLE WHISPER

Copyright © 1985 by
The C.S.S. Publishing Company, Inc.
Lima, Ohio

All rights reserved. No portion of this book may be reproduced or utilized in any form or by any means, electronic or mechanical including photocopying, without permission in writing from the publisher. Inquiries should be addressed to: The C.S.S. Publishing Company, Inc., 628 South Main Street, Lima, Ohio 45804.

5858/ISBN 0-89536-752-1   PRINTED IN U.S.A.

To Lee,
whom God placed in my life
to deepen my understanding and experience
of the Christ within

Table of Contents

A Note Concerning Lectionaries and Calendars   9

Preface   11

About the Title   13

The Day of Pentecost   *Finding Our Place*   15
Genesis 11:1-9

The Holy Trinity   *Travels With Wisdom*   19
Proverbs 8:22-31

Proper 4[1]
Pentecost 2[2]   *That All May Know Thee*   25
Corpus Christi[3]   *1 Kings 8:22-23, 41-43*

Proper 5
Pentecost 3   *Elijah — Man of Faith*   29
Ordinary Time 10   *1 Kings 17:17-24*

A sermon outside the lectionary cycle   *Letting God Work*   35
1 Kings 18
(for pastors who wish to preach a series on Elijah)

Proper 6
Pentecost 4   *The Desert of Discouragement*   41
Ordinary Time 11   *1 Kings 19:1-8*

Proper 7
Pentecost 5   *The Gentle Whisper*   45
Ordinary Time 12   *1 Kings 19:9-14*

Proper 8
Penetecost 6   *Our Higher Calling*   51
Ordinary Time 13   *1 Kings 19:15-21*

[1] Common Lectionary
[2] Lutheran Lectionary
[3] Roman Catholic Lectionary

Proper 9
Pentecost 7
Ordinary Time 14

The Interrupter 55
1 Kings 21:1-3, 17-21

Proper 10
Pentecost 8
Ordinary Time 15

Ascension Power 61
2 Kings 2:1, 6-14

Proper 11
Pentecost 9
Ordinary Time 16

The Risk of Life 67
2 Kings 4:8-17

The following index will aid the user of this book in matching the right Sunday with the appropriate text during the second half of the church year. Days listed here include only those appropriate to the contents of this book:

Fixed-date Lectionaries

Common	*Roman Catholic*	*Lutheran Lectionary*
Proper 4 *May 29—June 4*	Corpus Christi	Pentecost 2
Proper 5 *June 5-11*	Ordinary Time 10	Pentecost 3
Proper 6 *June 12-18*	Ordinary Time 11	Pentecost 4
Proper 7 *June 19-25*	Ordinary Time 12	Pentecost 5
Proper 8 *June 26—July 2*	Ordinary Time 13	Pentecost 6
Proper 9 *July 3-9*	Ordinary Time 14	Pentecost 7
Proper 10 *July 10-16*	Ordinary Time 15	Pentecost 8
Proper 11 *July 17-23*	Ordinary Time 16	Pentecost 9

Preface

All preaching is seasonal. Even when a sermon does not fall into a particular liturgical season, it still arises out of another season — the particular season in which the preacher finds himself when he is preaching a given sermon.

I wrote and preached the sermons that constitute this book in a season of personal and spiritual discovery. At the time these sermons were written, a number of factors in my life coincided to give me a new thirst for understanding and experiencing the mystery of union with Christ. The background of all these sermons is Paul's staggering affirmation that "it is no longer I who lives, but Christ who lives in me."

The discipline of preaching eleven Old Testament sermons at a time when I was personally struggling anew with the New Testament reality of life in Christ provided an interesting challenge. I found myself looking at these passages, and particularly at Elijah, not just in themselves, but through the lens of Christ's work of salvation and living presence within.

This approach proved, in my judgment, to be a valuable and enlightening way to unfold the message of these passages, not only in their original context but also in their fullest context — the Christ in whom all things hold together.

— Duane Kelderman

About The Title

The greatest realities of life are invisible. "The wind blows wherever it pleases," Jesus says. "You hear its sound, but you cannot tell where it comes from or where it is going. So it is with everyone born of the Spirit." Every Pentecost preacher knows this is true, though even in a lifetime we will not fully understand it.

Elijah discovered the power of the invisible God when he went to Mount Horeb, seeking some word from above. After a driving storm, a fearful earthquake, and a blazing fire, God finally spoke — in a gentle whisper (1 Kings 19:12). In the gentle whisper Elijah apprehended the breathtaking majesty and gentleness of God.

Pentecost is the season in which we as preachers most seek to tune people's ears to hearing God's gentle whisper. That is no easy task in a culture where silence is fearfully avoided, and where our senses have become addicted to stimulating sights and sounds all around us.

Perhaps the place for us to begin is to walk with Elijah up Mount Horeb, allow all the sights and sounds of falling rocks and blazing fire to pass, and then listen . . . for the gentle whisper.

Genesis 11:1-9 　　　　　　　　　　　The Day of Pentecost

Finding Our Place

One of my finest pastimes as a child was building forts. The house we lived in had a creek running through the back yard and on out through several vacant lots and a field. Along the creek were many trees. I would hate to guess how many forts my friend David and I built in those trees — *per week!* Carpenters in town would see us coming, and knew that we were there to ask if we could scrounge through their scrap piles for some boards to use for constructing these architectural nightmares.

The architecture notwithstanding, forts were wonderful things. They were places we could call our own. No one else could come in our fort. True, most of the time there were so many gaping holes in them that you didn't know whether you were inside or outside. But that didn't matter. The fort was *our place.* And we made sure everyone in the neighborhood knew that.

Building forts is nothing new. Our text today gives us the record of humankind's earliest attempts to find security and fellowship in a fort made with human hands. Fear lies behind the construction of this tower of Babel. "We need a place that we can call our own," they say. "We'll build a tower and a city, and we'll make a name for ourselves. And it will keep us together." Their reasons for building this tower make clear a lingering sense of separation, of disconnectedness, a sense of incompleteness that they thought would be satisfied if they could just have a place they could call theirs.

We have not stopped building forts and towers. In our natural condition, we continue to feel, quite correctly, that not all is well. That nagging fear of rejection, that subtle loneliness, that sense that our life just isn't quite complete, drives us into building towers —

to give us the illusion of security and community.

Our towers may be our possessions. They give us something concrete by which we can identify ourselves and relate to others. Our towers may be our good looks. We try to find inner peace and try to build the semblance of relationships by just putting a good wrapping around ourselves. Our towers may be our natural talents. We have a lot of them, and we can do a pretty good job of holding our life together. We have our careers, our goals which define our life and our relationships. Our towers may be our addictions or our obsessions that, in their own distorted way, give a semblance of wellbeing. Our towers may be our prejudices and the perverted sense of security they give us. Whatever our towers, they often "work" for us for a long time. The illusion they create — that life is okay — is a powerful one.

God recognizes the powerful way these towers can function in our lives. In fact, he says (Genesis 11:6) that something has to be done about this tower on the plains of Shinar. For if these people complete this tower and city, "then nothing they plan to do will be impossible for them." God recognized the deceptive power that this tower and city had to create the illusion of security, community, and power.

So he confounds the language of these people so that they cannot complete the tower. And they scatter over the face of the earth.

THIS ACTION of God, all by itself, seems a bit negative, to say the least, and perhaps even a bit nasty. But God does more than just shatter their illusion of power and unity.

In the fullness of time, God comes to his world in his Son, Jesus Christ, and announces a new building program. He offers a totally new and wonderfully different place where the human person will find meaning and security. This new place is not a physical building that will eventually crumble. It is a spiritual house whose cornerstone is Jesus Christ. Peter says that when we put our trust in Jesus Christ for our salvation and surrender our life to him, we each become living stones in that spiritual house. Paul says, "In Christ the whole building (comprised of people who are one with Christ by faith) is joined together and rises to become a holy temple in the Lord."

Not only does God announce a new building program. On Pentecost Day, God announces a new language. The Holy Spirit descends upon that crowd in Jerusalem, and people from every nation under heaven hear every other person speaking to them in their own language. The confusion of Babel is replaced by a language that Paul, in 1 Corinthians 2, says is not of this world but is of the Spirit. Its vocabulary is not learned by human wisdom, but is taught by the Spirit.

No, God doesn't just shatter our illusion of well-being and leave us scattered and confused. He offers us Christ. He offers us peace with God, which is what we seek with all of our fragile towers. He offers us eternal fellowship with Christ, and with any other person who has also found his or her place, not in his or her towers or in his or herself, but in Christ.

EACH ONE OF US would do well to place ourselves in this chain of events. Are you still out on the plains of Shinar, desperately building towers, seeking security and fullness in that which will always, always eventually crumble? Or have you walked up the hill of Calvary and found your place with Christ — not just watching him die, but dying with him — and discovering that life is not *building* our towers but *being built up* into Jesus Christ?

We would rather not have to choose between the tower and the cross. Isn't there some middle ground between the plains of Shinar and the hill of Calvary? Can't we find some security and fulfillment in our own efforts, in our own accomplishments, in our own towers, so long as we keep in mind that Christ is the one who somehow makes it all complete?

There is something deep in the human spirit that wants the best of both worlds. We want Christ, but don't want to let go of what we already have. But that is not the nature of life in Christ and in the Spirit. There is no common ground between the brick of Babel and the living stones of God's spiritual house. Jesus tells Nicodemus that there can be no blending together of flesh and Spirit. You must die to the order of flesh and be born anew into the order of the Spirit. There is no adding together of human effort and Christ's.

Christ did not die and rise again to add something to our life, to give a new face to the tower of Babel. He wants to *be* our life. He did not send his Spirit to influence us. The Spirit descends on this Pentecost Day to transform us.

Some of you are tired — tired of hacking it out on the plains of Shinar. You build your towers and cities, but they never deliver what they seemed to promise. Why don't you lay down your trowel and shovel, and while you're laying things down, lay down your life only to discover that it is no longer you who lives but Christ who lives in you.

Fix your sight upon that city whose maker and builder is God. Yes, Christ not only offers a new building, a new language, but the promise of a new city. John saw that city coming down out of heaven. As that city unfolds before his eyes, a voice cries from heaven, "Now the dwelling of God is with men, and he will live with them. They will be his people, and God himself will be with them and be their God. He will wipe every tear from their eyes. There will be no more death or mourning or crying or pain, for the old order of things has passed away."

Yes, we are the living stones that are part of a new, eternal city. Let the transient towers of sin and self crumble. Let the old order of things pass away. Experience the new order of things. Be built into that which is eternal. Find your place — in Jesus.

Proverbs 8:22-31 *Trinity Sunday*

Travels With Wisdom

I would like to introduce you to someone today. You may have never met her. In fact, you may have never even heard of her. She is a biblical character. Her name is "Wisdom." You have maybe read about her before in the book of Proverbs. She is always calling people to listen to her and follow her advice.

Wisdom is a difficult person to understand. At first, we think she's a person. Throughout the book of Proverbs, Wisdom is referred to with words like "she" and "her." Yet wisdom is not so much a real person as a principle of life, a dimension of God, a feature of God's creation. At first glance, Wisdom seems to have existed before the world began. Yet we know that no one except God existed before his creation of the world. At one time she seems to be God himself, but at other times, she clearly exists apart from God.

I'd like to ask you to set aside all of those big, abstract questions about Wisdom today, and just think of her the way Proverbs tells us to — as a person. If you can do that, the questions we have about her won't seem so important. In fact, when you get to know Wisdom a little better, you won't even think that much about Wisdom herself. She gets you thinking about God, and about the kind of world he has made.

WISDOM WAS a very popular person in ancient times. Everyone liked to talk about her and what she stood for. Just pick something that you really enjoy talking about. Maybe you're a sports nut and like to talk about your favorite football team, or the baseball team you think will win the pennant. You can go for hours talking about sports. Or maybe you've recently purchased a computer, and find yourself fascinated with this whole new world and can go on for hours with someone else who has done the same and has similar interests.

In ancient times, people loved to sit around and talk about Wisdom. Wisdom was the source of insight. She was the beginning of knowledge. She was understanding. To talk about wisdom was to talk about basic issues of truth and justice. Getting to know Wisdom better made you a more discerning, disciplined person. It got you more in touch with the heartbeat of the universe.

Just consider a couple of Wisdom's saying and you can see why she was so interesting:

> *A little sleep, a little slumber, a little folding of the hands to rest — and poverty will come on you like a bandit and scarcity like an armed man. (Proverbs 6:10-11)*
>
> *For the lips of an adultress drip honey, and her speech is smoother than oil; but in the end she is bitter as gall, sharp as a double-edged sword. (Proverbs 5:3-4)*

Wisdom's words were always provocative. And they were never unrelated to real life. She was not some idle dreamer. Her words always grabbed her listeners right where they lived. Those ancient people didn't always like what Wisdom had to say. And they certainly didn't always obey her. But they could sit a whole night around a campfire trying to sharpen their minds and focus their wills as they considered her insights.

GIVEN THAT general introduction to Wisdom, we are now ready to narrow our focus to today's text. Of all the biblical material on this intriguing woman, Proverbs 8:22-31 lifts her to her greatest heights. These verses tell us of Wisdom's greatest moment: when she was with God as he created the world. These verses tell us two things about Wisdom, and more importantly, about the world God created.

1. An Ordered Creation

First, Wisdom is *the witness to an ordered creation*. Wisdom, the symbol of order, knowledge, and truth, was with God when he created the world. "The Lord possessed me at the beginning of his work, before his deeds of old; I was appointed from eternity, from the beginning, before the world began." (vv. 22-23) And in verse 30 she describes her role in creation: "I was the craftsman at his side."

Wisdom tells us today, "This world in which we live is not just some jumbled assembly of molecules and protoplasm. It is a world shot through with order, with design, with deep wisdom and meaning. It is the splendid handiwork of an intelligent and personal creator. I know because I was there when God created this world and was the craftsman at his side."

There are two ways to view the world in which we live. These two ways can be illustrated by a cabinet I have in my garage. On my tool bench I have a blue box with twenty four little drawers in it. In each of these different drawers I have different sizes of wood screws, different sizes of sheet metal screws, nails of different lengths and thicknesses, and nuts and bolts that are different lengths and widths. They are all neatly arranged in different drawers.

One view of God's creation is to say that God just took all these different drawers and dumped their contents into one pile. There is no order, no design. He just threw it all together, and our task as human beings is to try to bring order to this jumbled mess. The task of science, in this view of the world, is to try to make order out of chaos.

But Wisdom gives us quite a different picture of creation, more along the lines of the different drawers I have for everything in my garage. Creation is orderly. Everything is in its exact place. There is design to this world. Our task as human beings is not to try to give order to the world, but to *discover* the beautiful order that already exists by virtue of God's orderly, intelligent creation.

It's in keeping with the orderly design of creation that God says to Adam in Genesis 1:28, "Subdue the earth." That is, take the wonderful creation I have given you and unfold its beauty, put it to use, build things with its wonderful resources. Uncover the wonder and power of nature. And in so doing, you will discover the magnificent design and wisdom of the creator.

There's one more thing we must add to this first truth about Wisdom. Wisdom is the witness to an ordered creation *which stirs our hearts to praise God!* Wisdom herself bubbles over with joy and praise as she sees this wonderful creation of God unfold before her very eyes.

> *I was filled with delight day after day, rejoicing always in his presence, rejoicing in his whole world and delighting in mankind."*
> (v. 30)

She's having the time of her life! She watches as God measures off the horizon, and puts the clouds in place, and marks the boundary of the sea. And every time God does something, her heart just heaves with delight. "God, this is just unbelievable!" She is filled with praise to God.

Today, these thousands or millions of years later, we still bow down in praise to God at the splendor of his creation. We still sing those strong words of the hymnwriter:

> *This is my Father's world, and to my listening ears*
> *All nature sings, and round me rings the music of the spheres!*

And the words of the Psalmist still ring in our hearts:

> *The heavens declare the glory of God;*
> *the skies proclaim the work of his hands.*

2. A Moral Creation

There is a second thing that we learn about Wisdom from Proverbs 8. Not only is she the witness to an ordered creation which stirs our hearts to praise God; she is *the voice of a moral creation that stirs our wills to obey God.*

Wisdom is a voice that constantly calls people to listen to her and to follow her. For she knows something else about God's creation. She is the witness to the deep *moral fabric* of the universe. She knows, because she was there when God created this world with certain unchanging moral boundaries. And she knows that those moral boundaries cannot be violated without doing injury to ourselves and those around us. So she now also stirs our wills to obey God, to fall in line with the moral rhythm of the universe.

In modern language she is saying, "Listen, my friends, I was with God when he made this world. And when I call you to 'do this' or 'not do this,' I'm not just guessing about what is the best and wisest way to live. I know that God's commandments — every one of them — fit with how he made this world. This world has deep within it certain deep and unchanging moral contours. You can try to ignore them or change them, but it will never work."

Just take one of the moral contours of this world that just can't be changed. Wisdom says in Proverbs 17:9, "He who covers over an offense promotes love, but whoever repeats the matter separates close friends." My hunch is that we have all experienced the truth of this proverb in our own lives. We have experienced the peace of mind that comes from not repeating someone's wrongdoing and affirming what is positive in that person. We have probably also experienced the opposite situation. We repeat something that doesn't need to be repeated, and there is a rupture in the relationship. A close friendship is deeply injured.

Wisdom is telling us that we can try to ignore (in this case) "love" as a basic moral contour to this universe. And we may think that we can sidestep that call to love in our relationships, and carelessly repeat offenses whenever it pleases us. But we cannot do that without sooner or later injuring someone. Wisdom says, "I was there. I know how God made this world. Do yourself a favor and obey God, keep his commandments, listen to my insights into how life works, and how it doesn't work."

I think of the things that Wisdom has to say to us about adultery about truth, about stealing, about injustice, about the peril of riches. These things were written nearly 3,000 years ago. Yet they are as true today as they were then. And that's because Wisdom isn't just giving us her opinions. She is revealing to us an unchanging moral structure to the universe that has existed from the beginning.

THE FACT IS, however, that wisdom can only *stir* our wills to obey God. She cannot transform our wills. She can teach us the moral contours of the universe. But knowledge alone does not make us abide by those contours. To be able to truly obey God, we need to know someone else, who has a faint resemblance to Wisdom, but who is very different. That someone is Jesus Christ.

Commentators have often noted the resemblance of our friend Wisdom and our Savior, Jesus Christ. There are some interesting parallels. John tells us that Christ was with God in the beginning, and that through Christ all things were made. And Paul says (in Colossians 1:16) that "in Christ all things were created, in heaven and on earth . . . all things were created through him and for him." And in Colossians 2:3, Christ is the one "in whom are hid all the treasures of *wisdom* and knowledge." The resemblance between these two characters is interesting.

But whether or not there is some kind of literary thread between Wisdom and Christ is not as important as realizing this: before we can truly heed Wisdom's words, we must experience Christ's renewing power. We must know his forgiving grace, that which sets us free from the guilt of sin. And we must experience his resurrection power that sets us free from the power of sin. Without our death to the old order of things, and our resurrection to a new order — the order of the Spirit — we will only *hear* Wisdom's words, and at best, sporadically try to follow them. But when we have died to sin and have risen to Christ, and live in the Spirit of Pentecost, we cannot only hear, but joyfully *follow* her ways.

THERE YOU HAVE her: Wisdom, the witness to an ordered creation, the voice of a moral creation. Get to know Wisdom better. Become her friend. Listen to her tell of the wonder of God's creation, and praise God! Listen to her tell of the moral contours of God's creation, and with the power of Christ and his Spirit within you, obey God!

1 Kings 8:22-23; 41-43

Proper 4
Pentecost 2
Corpus Christi

That All May Know Thee

What a day this must have been in the life of Israel! The dedication of the Temple! Many years had already gone by since God had given his blessing upon the idea of building a temple like this — many years of waiting, and then many years of building this magnificent structure. And now the day has finally come. It's time to carefully place the Ark of the Covenant, which had been the symbol of God's divine presence for so many years, into the inner sanctuary of the Temple. The priest's lower the Ark, which contained the two tablets of the law given to Moses on Mount Sinai, beneath the wings of the cherubim. And as they turn around to come out, a cloud fills the temple. The glory of the Lord has now filled this place!

Even as this cloud engulfs the temple, Solomon stands outside before all the people and prays this prayer of dedication that constitutes our text today.

The part of the prayer that we're considering today is actually only one of six parts to this prayer. But it may be the most intriguing and unexpected part. It is a prayer for the foreigner. The Old Testament talks frequently about the "foreigner." Sometimes he is called the "alien," or "stranger," or "sojourner." All of those words roughly refer to that person who was not a Jew, who was not a part of the seed of Abraham or the theocratic kingdom of Israel.

One of the common misconceptions of modern Christians is that God did not care much about the foreigner in the Old Testament era. The fact is that God constantly reminded the Jews that while they were his special, chosen people, destined to have a special role in ushering in the kingdom of God through Jesus Christ, they were always to show compassion to the foreigner. Although there were many privileges that foreigners did not enjoy, it is instructive to look at the Old Testament and see how many protections and basic human rights and even privileges God did give to the foreigner. He often reminds the people of Israel that *they* themselves were once foreigners in Egypt.

To this day God has a heart for the foreigner, for the outsider, the person who doesn't fit. God has a special place in his heart for those whose rights are trampled upon by a presuming majority. Throughout his earthly ministry, Jesus identifies with those people who never quite "made it" by the social standards of that day.

WHAT DOES SOLOMON pray regarding these foreigners? He pleads with God to hear the prayers of those foreigners who will come to this temple, and to do what they ask of him. And why does he want God to do those things? "In order that all the peoples of the earth may know thy name and fear thee."

Solomon's desires could have been completely different. It certainly would have been easy for Solomon to seek fame and glory for himself on this historic day. After all, he was the king under whose reign this masterpiece was constructed. He was the master architect and the master planner. In purely human terms, this was Solomon's day.

Or his desires could have been that his children and his children's children would know God. Could't a large dose of Jewish nationalism be excused on this great day? After all, look what the Jews had to endure from foreigners to get to this great day?

Solomon's prayer is neither focused upon himself nor upon his "own people." He prays that "all the peoples of the earth" may know and fear God's name.

Now we shouldn't think that Solomon came to such lofty aspirations easily. The book of Ecclesiastes is the story of Solomon's pursuit of happiness through self-fulfillment and self-indulgence. The fact is that Solomon first tried all the ways to happiness that focus upon the self. He gave himself to pleasure, to riches, to wisdom, to power and fame. But none of those things gave any lasting happiness, any lasting joy. They are all ultimately vain, he concludes, because they focus upon the self, and the self will eventually die. He concludes that the only worthy and fulfilling end of man is to fear God and keep his commandments. And, in keeping with that end, Solomon now prays that this temple will be a vehicle which God uses to further the glory and fear of *his* name.

THAT LEADS US to the third thing we need to look at in this passage. We've looked at the person for whom Solomon is praying (the foreigner). We've looked at the content of his prayer (that *all* people would know God). Finally, we observe *how* Solomon expects that prayer to be answered.

How will it happen that people coming to this temple will know God? Won't they just be struck at the grandeur and beauty of the structure? No, this was much more than a building. It was the dwelling place of God. In the beginning of his prayer, as the cloud of God's glory still hangs behind him, Solomon stands in awe that God actually dwells in this temple.

> "But will God really dwell on earth? The heavens, even the highest heaven, cannot contain you. How much less this temple I have built!" (v. 27)

But in some mysterious way, God *did* dwell in the inner sanctuary of this temple. And people who would come to this place from the far corners of the earth would not just see a beautiful structure. They would see the glory of God.

SOLOMON'S TEMPLE is no longer the dwelling place of God. In the later days, God came in Jesus Christ. And Christ, in his death and resurrection, was the temple that was destroyed and rebuilt again in three days. In Christ dwelt all the fullness of God.

But where is the temple now? The temple of Solomon and several subsequent temples have long been leveled. Christ has long been ascended into heaven. Where is the temple *now*? Where does God dwell now? Paul answers our question: "Don't you know that you yourselves are God's temple and that God's Spirit lives in you?" (1 Corinthians 3:16)

And of all of us together Paul says, "In Christ you too are being built together to become a dwelling in which God lives by his Spirit." (Ephesians 2:22) Each of us individually, and we together as a community of faith, *are* the temple, the dwelling place of God.

The question today is: Do people, when they see us, come to see the cloud of God's glory? Do they come to know God? What do people see when they see us? Do they just see a body and a personality or do they in some mysterious way see through that fragile vessel to God's Spirit who is within us and is being released through us?

When "outsiders" see us together as a community of faith, what do they see? Do they simply see a group of people whose common characteristics, such as race, educational level, and socio-economic class, create natural barriers to outsiders? Or do they experience that mysterious principle of spiritual inclusion that is at work in the body of Christ, that principle by which, according to Paul in Ephesians 2:19, there are no longer foreigners and aliens, but all are now fellow citizens?

Solomon's desire was that all the peoples of the earth would know God. But people will only know God by what they see in us.

I was talking recently to a person who has been visiting our church. I asked her how she came in contact with the church. "Well," she said, "we sent our son to your preschool. But we ran into some financial problems in our family, and after months of just barely being able to scratch up the money to send our son to your preschool, we finally couldn't come up with the money last spring. There were two months left in preschool, so we called up Wanda and Claire, the preschool directors, and told them that our son wasn't going to be coming in any more. And I explained why. Wanda said, 'You send your son to school. We'll worry about that other stuff later. You just send you son to preschool.' " The mother told me that after she was done crying a couple days later, she said to herself, "You know, I think I'd like to go and see what that church is all about." The parents are presently in the process of joining this fellowship.

We are the temple of God, his dwelling place. People no longer have to travel on the back of a donkey over mountain ridges and long dusty trails to see the temple of God. They just have to look at us.

What do they see? I hope they see people who love, who care, who listen, people who have an unusual poise and glory about them, because it is not they who live but Christ who lives in them.

You are the dwelling place of God. May you be God's vessel, God's instrument through which all the peoples of the earth will know his name.

2 Kings 17:17-24 Proper 5
Pentecost 3
Ordinary Time 10

Elijah — Man of Faith

With each new presidential campaign season, we again get a firsthand glimpse of some of the pressures of being a national leader. Whatever opinion we may have of a particular candidate, we can't help but be impressed with the stamina he or she needs if he or she aspires to lead a nation as diverse as our own.

How must it feel to lead a party when barely over *50 percent* of your own party members voted for you and what you stand for? It's always been amazing to me that presidents usually lead this nation with a less than *50 percent* of the populace approving of what they do. It takes tremendous endurance and stamina.

Elijah's task, however, makes even the job of being president look very manageable. At least the president can take solace in the fact that on one particular day in November, a plurality of people judged that he would make a better president than one other person. Elijah was called to be a leader of Israel when virtually no one wanted to hear what he had to say.

Ahab was the king when Elijah prophesied. Ahab had the dubious distinction of having done "more evil in the eyes of the Lord than any before him." (1 Kings 16:30) Ahab and his wife Jezebel had sold out to the worship of Baal, a false god, the god of the Canaanites. They had recently built a great temple to Baal in Samaria, along with an altar and the Asherah pole, important symbols in the worship of Baal.

Into that situation God now calls Elijah to go and proclaim the word of the living God. I'd like to look today at Elijah *as a man of faith,* a man who, against tremendous odds, trusted God, took

God at his word, and acted upon it. Whether it was believing that indeed God would dry up the heavens for several years and feed him in the meantime, or believing that God would indeed provide food and drink for a poor widow, or believing that God could and would raise this widow's son from the dead, Elijah, in this seventeenth chapter of 1 Kings, stands as a man of unshakable faith in God.

IT'S IMPORTANT TO SEE, in the first place, the *source,* the basis of Elijah's faith, What makes it possible for Elijah to believe these outrageous claims of what God would do? The source of Elijah's faith had nothing to do with himself. It wasn't his raw intelligence. It wasn't his great wisdom or ingenuity. It was rather the absolute reliability and faithfulness of God.

Elijah simply believed that God indeed was God, and could do and would do exactly what he said. He actually believed that when God said he would defy all the laws of nature and make it stop raining, he would do just that. He believed that God would feed him at the ravine of Kerith. God laid out the menu in verse 4:1, "You will drink from the brook, and I have ordered the ravens to feed you there." And, in verse 5, we read these simple but astounding words: "So he (Elijah) did what the Lord had told him."

And when he encounters the widow of Zarephath, he has so much confidence in the word of God that he tells her, without batting an eye, that one little jar of flour and jug of oil in her kitchen will never empty out until the famine is over.

And when her boy dies, Elijah throws himself totally upon the faithfulness of God to raise this boy. And God does just that.

The source of our faith, too, is nothing less than the absolute reliability and faithfulness of God. Is there an area in your life in which you are anxious? God says that he will take care of the birds of the air and the lilies of the field, and that if he takes care of them, he will certainly take care of you. Do you believe him?

Are you struggling with temptation today? Are you wavering, knowing what you should do, but doubting whether you can follow through? Do you believe God's Word when it says that we are no longer slaves to sin, that sin no longer has dominion over us, and that we have at our disposal the power of God which was exerted when he raised Christ from the dead? Do you believe that?

Are you doubting this morning whether you can stick it out in your marriage? You say, "I'm not sure I have enough in me to love my wife or husband any more." You're right. You don't. But is *your strength* what gives hope to your marriage? Or is it the Spirit of God, whom we trust to enable us to love with Christ's love, to forgive with Christ's compassion, to wait with Christ's patience? The entire Christian walk is a walk of faith. It is a walk of trusting, not just for salvation but for every act, every decision, every commitment, in the promises and provision of God.

The source of Elijah's faith was nothing less than the absolute reliability of God in fulfilling his Word.

THAT LEADS US to look, in the second place, at the *cultivation* of Elijah's faith. How did God cultivate and develop Elijah's faith? In a nutshell, he cast him into the only situation in which we ever learn to trust God — a situation of total dependence.

Think about it. God certainly didn't have to send Elijah to a creek for two years. For so long a period of time, he could have had Elijah walk for a few more days to a place where he didn't have to . . . didn't have to what? . . . totally trust in God, day by day, for over 700 days, to provide water in the brook, and a raven who would come by and drop off something to eat. For over two years, God sent Elijah to school — the school of faith, a situation in which Elijah learned to depend totally upon God. And God always met his needs.

The fact is that the only way we learn to trust in God is through situations where everything else in which we are tempted to trust has been stripped away. Today God has some of us sitting down by the creek with Elijah. We don't know what the future holds for us. We're living a day at a time. Perhaps we don't know if the pain in our body will ever go away. You don't know if you'll have your job next month. You don't know whether you'll *get* a job by next month. You feel powerless over your circumstances. There's really nothing you can do . . . except trust in God. That's called *school:* the school of faith.

I can hear some of you saying, "I'd like to drop out of school." That's an understandable feeling. But the fact is that God, in his unfathomable wisdom, has us enrolled. Sit by the creek, beside Elijah, and learn the painful, liberating art of trusting, totally trusting, moment by moment, day by day, in the faithfulness of God.

FINALLY, WE LEARN something not only about the *source* of our faith, and the *cultivation* of our faith, but also something about the *reward* of faith. When we totally put our trust in God, the reward, quite simply, is that we experience the faithfulness of God.

Paul says in Philippians 4:19, "And my God will meet *all* your needs according to his glorious riches in Christ Jesus." When Paul wrote these words, he wasn't passing on some theory he had read in a book. He was writing from a prison cell!

Faith has this wonderful way of feeding upon itself. The more we step out in total trust in God, the more we experience his faithfulness, no matter what the circumstances of our life. By our standards of prosperity Elijah probably shouldn't have gotten too excited about God's faithfulness. He didn't even have enough food for tomorrow, not to mention a microwave in which to cook it. But Elijah, along a creekside, like Paul in a prison, knew that God was faithful. And that knowledge, deep in his soul, was its own reward.

Several years ago, I worked with a beautiful person named Debi, a thirty-year-old who has diabetes and is already fighting for her eyesight. She is bound to kidney dialysis because of kidneys that don't work any more, has already had one transplant that failed and that almost took her life, and now is facing the prospect of another transplant attempt. Add to all of that that she has just one sibling, a brother, and he is in worse shape than she, as he is dying a slow death to cancer.

Recently I received a letter from Debi. I'd like you to listen to some parts of it.

> *I am really happy that I managed to teach the whole year. At the beginning of the year Ed and I both had some doubts that I would be able to pull it off, especially when I came down with peritonitis (an infection resulting from kidney dialysis) the very first day of school. I was hospitalized then and a few more times with another case of peritonitis, hernia surgery, and a catheter removal, but I stuck it out without too much difficulty. Near the end of the school year I developed another infection, and the peritoneal catheter had to come out, so I finished up the year on hemodialysis and got along just fine with it.*
>
> *Dave has been having a lot of problems lately. His right arm and hand have been permanently paralyzed, and for a few months his other arm and both legs began to be very weak, but the doctors located a tumor growing along his spine and zapped it with radiation in time to prevent any lasting damage. Then he began having*

> *terrible back pains, and they found that his left kidney has a large tumor in it. Right now he is in the hospital, but he may be home soon.*

If Elijah was enrolled in the college of faith, then this brother and sister, I think we would all agree, are at least in college, if not in graduate school. But listen now to what she writes about the reward of total trust in God:

> *Dave and I are closer than ever. We both understand that life, even with its restrictions, is wonderful, and each day is a gift from God, and death will not be the worst thing that can happen to us. We're so happy that when the time comes, we know that one of us will be able to help the other let go. Until then, each day is a precious gift from God, and is wonderful.*

A brother and a sister, holding each other's hand on the slippery edge of life itself, do not testify to the faithfulness of God and the goodness of life in God's world because they thought that would be a good technique for coping with their situation! They testify to this faithfulness of God because they have *experienced it*, because they have put all of their trust and hope in God and God alone.

Yes, the more purely we trust in God, the more we experience his trustworthiness, his peace; the more we see that life, no matter what the circumstances, is good — because God is good. God is faithful. God is love.

I'm not sure where you are sitting today, whether it's at the creekside beside Elijah, or on the mountaintop where Elijah spent an afternoon with Jesus and Moses. But it really doesn't matter. For whether Elijah was sitting at the creekside or on the mountaintop, he knew and rested in one thing — *the faithfulness of God.*

God rules! God is faithful! God is good! God will never let you go. Nothing will separate you from his love. Live, today and every day, ever resting in the fact that we are not our own, but belong to that great and faithful God, through Jesus Christ our Lord.

1 Kings 18

Letting God Work

A sermon outside the lectionary cycle (for pastors who wish to preach a series on Elijah)

The lesson of this showdown at Mount Carmel is very simple: our God is truly God! He is the only God. He is the all-powerful God of heaven and earth. He is stronger than anyone else. He is stronger than any force of nature. He is stronger than any other "gods" that the human mind creates. As the people said, "The Lord — he is God."

And the point for us today, of course, is that this is not just Elijah's God. This is your God. This is my God. This God who consumed the altar on Mount Carmel still lives. He reigns. He rules.

I'd like to pose a question: "Where is Mount Carmel today?" How do we see this dramatic power of God today? How can we pit our God against the gods of this age and hear thousands cry, "The Lord — he is God." Where is the consuming fire of God today?

I'd like to point out three things that Elijah did that we must do if we are to reenact in our lives and in our day the drama of Mount Carmel.

First, *we must set up the test.* Elijah set up a very clear and unmistakable test of the power of God. He said, "One of these altars is going to start on fire, and one isn't." And then we'll know who is God. He didn't just give some kind of theological lecture. He didn't say, "You prophets of Baal are wrong; you really should believe in the Lord. I have the words of Moses here. Now you look at this and see if I'm not right." Instead he said, "It's time for a test — a test that we all agree will reveal to us who the real God is. Fire is going to come down upon one altar or the other!"

How many of us are willing to make *our lives* the test, the proof that God is real? How many of us are willing to gather together all those who would doubt that God really exists and makes a difference, and say, "Watch and see if my life isn't so different because Christ is in me that there can be no doubt that God is real, that God makes a difference?"

Elijah was willing to put everything to the test, And Christ demands no less of us. Christ says, "You are either for me or against me — no middle ground. You either serve God or money — no middle ground, You either bear fruit, or you don't bear fruit — no middle ground. You either love your neighbor, or you hate him — no middle ground. You either are in the light or you are in the darkness — no middle ground. Nicodemus, you either live in the flesh, or you are born again and you live in the Spirit — no middle ground. You're either hot or cold — no lukewarm middle ground."

Now, we don't like such clear lines in life. We're not comfortable with such clear tests of God's power. If I were on Mount Carmel, I'd probably be tempted to make sure that the altars were close enough together so that whatever happened, no one could either claim a clear victory or be faced with clear defeat. It's easier to live in spiritual mediocrity and forego the drama of Mount Carmel, than to live in spiritual power and call the gods of the world to their knees.

Yet there is another side of us that really does want to reach higher, that wants to know the power of Christ that Paul talks about. There is a side of us that's tired of shaving off the cutting edge of Paul's call to be holy, and blameless. We wonder with eager longing what it would be like to be conformed to the image of Jesus Christ. We want to see the kingdom of God in the earth.

But we don't want to make a fool out of God, much less ourselves. So we really never take the risk, set up the test, put ourselves on the line. We talk ourselves into a Christian walk that has no power, into a gospel that consoles us in defeat, but does not lead us to expect a real difference in our lives. We cancel the test at Mount Carmel.

The first thing we must do if we are to see Mount Carmel today is set up the test.

2.

Secondly, *we must trust that the victory is ours.* Elijah never doubted what the outcome of this test on Mount Carmel would be. He plays with the prophets of Baal. He taunts them, "Shout a little louder. Maybe he can't hear you. Maybe he's gone on a trip. Maybe he's sleeping." The Living Bible says, "Maybe he's out sitting on the toilet." Elijah has total confidence that their gods will fail them.

And when it's his turn, he is so confident that the true God will deliver fire down upon the altar that he takes twelve buckets of water and totally drenches the altar just so that there's no question about what really happened.

Some of you might be saying, "But I don't have that much confidence in myself. I wouldn't dare set myself up as the proof of God's power." Well, you're on the right track. Paul says, we ought to have no confidence in ourselves. In Philippians 3, he lists all the things he could cite to build himself up, and he says, "I consider all of those things *rubbish,* that I may gain Christ and *be found in him."*

My friends, we have a confidence, a reason to believe that the power of God can be displayed through us and in our day, such that makes Elijah look like a wild fool. The confidence we have, living in the power of the cross and resurrection of Jesus Christ, makes Elijah, *who didn't even know* Christ, look like some kind of spiritual Evel Knieval.

The cross is our basis for standing shoulder to shoulder beside Elijah wherever we live today. The fact is that Jesus Christ in his death took on Satan one-on-one, and in his resurrection disarmed Satan of his power. He crushed the head of the serpent. Hebrews says that Christ endured every possible temptation and snare of Satan and prevailed. For that reason, *we* can have confidence, not just confidence that we will be forgiven of our sins, but confidence that we can be delivered from sin and can withstand sin and defeat in our lives just like Christ did.

We can have that confidence because Christ not only *defeated Satan* at Calvary. He *freed us from Satan* at Calvary. We need to see exactly how he did that: not only did *Christ* die there in some mysterious way, *we* died there. In Romans 6 Paul says that sin no longer has any hold on us because we died to sin. Our old self was crucifed with Christ. And how can sin have a hold on something that's dead?

In Romans 7 Paul compares our relationship to sin with the marriage relationship. He says, when you are married, there is no way out of that relationship. You're bound to it. That's the promise you made before God. As one person put it, "You stick with who you're stuck with." In the same way, we, in our spiritual lives, are bound to a principle of sin that is a part of our fallen nature in Adam. And there is no way out of that bondage, just as when you are married, there's no way out of your marriage . . . unless the other person dies.

Well, Paul says, we were freed from the bondage of sin at Calvary because *we* died with Christ at Calvary. And when Christ arose, we arose to a new life with him. We are now in Christ — the victor. It is no longer I who lives, but Christ who lives in me. Paul concludes Romans 8 saying we are more than conquerors through Christ who loves us.

There is no question about whether God will deliver just one more Mount Carmel victory. He already has — in Jesus Christ. It is done. It is complete, totally accomplished.

3.

All we must do, indeed, all we *can* do (and that's the third thing Elijah shows us), is *let God work through us.* We must let the life of Christ, the vine, flow through us. We must let the Spirit of Christ fill us and control every action, every thought, and every word. And that requires a special posture, a special attitude.

Did you notice the difference in activity level between Elijah and the prophets of Baal? The prophets of Baal were themselves out trying to make a miracle happen. They've literally cut themselves in pieces trying to manufacture a victory for their god. Elijah calmly steps up, delivers a prayer of less than sixty words (he wasn't afflicted with a seminary education), steps aside, and watches God do his work. Paul says, "Offer yourselves *to God* as (his!) instruments of righteousness." When we see our whole life as being *in Christ,* we don't so much *act* as we let Christ act *through us.* We rest! We rest *in Christ.* Our life is the fruit of the Spirit's work in us and through us.

SOME OF YOU this morning are as tired as the prophets of Baal. You feel guilty about your mediocre walk with God, you live in constant spiritual defeat. You have tried to be more loving, more patient, more forgiving. You have tried to be less selfish. You have tried to truly love like Christ. But the more you try, the more you fail.

Why don't you say a simple prayer, of sixty words or less, and let God do his work — through you. Thank God for not only forgiving your sins, but for delivering you from your sin through his defeat of Satan on the cross and through our death with Christ to the power of sin. And then, quit trying to win some great spiritual victory for God that he has already won in Jesus Christ! Believe Hebrews when it says that the Christian life is a life of rest — rest in the completed victory of Jesus Christ. Jesus said long ago, "Come unto me, all you who labor and are heavy laden, and I will give you rest." He didn't say, "Come unto me and I'll give you the secret for winning the victory." He said, "Rest, rest in me, in what I will do for you and through you."

In Philippians 2 Paul says, "Work out your own salvation *with fear and trembling.*" Why with fear and trembling? *"For it is God who works in you* to will and to act according to his good purpose."

Do you want to see the drama of Mount Carmel reenacted in your life and in our day? Then set up the test; put yourself on the line. Trust in the accomplished victory of Jesus Christ. And let God do his work.

May all who see you say, "The Lord — he is God!"

1 Kings 19:1-8

Proper 6
Pentecost 4
Ordinary Time 11

The Desert of Discouragement

What a contrast between the Elijah we have observed the past two weeks and the Elijah in our text today! From the glory of Mount Carmel to the despondency of the broom tree. From the victorious showdown with the gods of Baal to a whimpering desire to die. In modern terms, it was like winning an Olympic gold medal one day, and calling the 911 suicide help line the next.

Elijah has had it. He is totally and unexpectedly unraveled by the threat of Jezebel. He runs away to Beersheeba and is so discouraged that he prays that the Lord will take his life.

I am afraid that possibilities abound for misinterpreting this passage and for missing the point of God for including this bitter chapter of Elijah's life in his written Word. One way to miss the point of this passage is to interpret this incident in Elijah's life as a totally negative experience, a time of meaningless failure in Elijah's life, simply a glaring chink in his moral armor. I'd like to suggest that more than that is going on here.

The opposite approach to this passage, which equally misses the point, is to simply console Elijah and ourselves under the broom tree, write off these times of discouragement as times that we all have once in a while (which, of course, we do), and simply wait for a better day.

Both the judgmental attitude and the sympathetic attitude have elements of truth in them; but they are superficial. They focus upon Elijah's behavior, but fail to see what God is doing with Elijah under the broom tree, and how God is at work in us when we go through the desert of discouragement.

I'd like to talk today about "the desert of discouragement." I'd like to suggest that the issue in discouragement, for Elijah and for us, is a subtle *loss of focus* that creeps into our soul, and that clouds from us the glorious truth about life in God's world, and life in Jesus Christ.

In two specific places in our text we see a subtle but devastating loss of focus on Elijah's part. First in verse 3 we read, "Elijah was afraid and ran for his life." Now many versions point out in the footnote on this verse that the original Hebrew here is very difficult to figure out, and that it could just as easily be translated, "Elijah *saw* (Jezebel) and ran for his life." However we translate it, the point of verse 3 is the same: Elijah is totally absorbed by Jezebel's threat and allows Jezebel and her threat on his life to totally control him. That's all he sees. Suddenly his vision of life narrows from the cosmic battle of Mount Carmel where God devastated Jezebel's forces (and where 450 prophets of Baal could have lynched Elijah after he showed them up, but where God protected him), to the angry threats of one evil woman. There is no proportion to Elijah's fears here. As rich as Elijah's faith had been, as richly as God had rewarded that faith, suddenly Elijah blocks all of that out. He is stricken with spiritual myopia.

How often doesn't our discouragement follow upon some specific incident that we have now allowed to take over the way we react to everything. One person says something to us or does something to us, or one thing goes wrong, and suddenly, all of life is bad. That's all we think about. We mull and brood over it. We make an even bigger deal out of it than it was. And we're very quickly in the desert and under the broom tree — discouraged.

It reminds me of the story of the young executive who came home totally dejected and discouraged at a bad turn of events at work that day. He said to his wife, "Honey, I'm a failure." To which she responded, "Oh, really! At the age of 25, you may be the world's youngest failure." We can easily lose all focus, all proportion in our life.

And what we have lost is our focus upon God, and upon his promises, his abiding presence, and his never-ending love. We block out all we know about the goodness and promises of God. We block out all the experiences in our own life of God's faithfulness. And suddenly all of life looks bleak.

THERE'S A SECOND, even more revealing, illustration of Elijah's loss of focus. In verse 4, Elijah says, "I have had enough, Lord. Take my life; I am no better than my ancestors." What an interesting confession, Did he at one time think that he *was* better than his ancestors? Somewhere between Mount Carmel and the broom tree, something happened to Elijah's view of his own place in God's work. His focus shifted from what *God* was doing to *himself* — how much better or worse he was, what his position was in all of this.

Now that shouldn't surprise us. There is nothing harder to handle in life than spiritual victory, success. When we experience some spiritual achievement, Satan's last recourse is to get us to shift the achievement from God's column to our column. And if he can subtly move God out of the picture, we are set up for discouragement. For without God, we had better run for our lives!

One eighteenth century saint said that all discouragement is disenchanted egotism. If we make ourselves the focus in our spiritual battles, and ourselves the star in our spiritual accomplishments, it's only a matter of time before we will be devastated.

How many ministers and Christian leaders have plunged down to defeat when they confused God's cause and their own cause, when they confused God's blessing and their achievement? When that subtle shift takes place, we suddenly find ourselves defending and protecting and controlling what has now become *our* cause instead of freely allowing God to work through us however *he* wills. The second we focus upon ourselves instead of upon God, we have set ourselves up for defeat and discouragement. That's what Elijah does. And with one reckless threat, Jezebel blew him away.

WE'VE LOOKED now at Elijah's loss of focus. What does God do about this situation? He first ministers to Elijah through an angel who feeds Elijah two times. Then God sends Elijah on a journey to Mount Horeb (Mount Sinai), a journey which, significantly, lasted forty days and forty nights.

Forty days and forty nights (or forty years) in the Scripture often indicates a period of testing, of purging, of deprivation so that God can once again be focused upon. Israel wanders in the wilderness for forty years before she is ready to enter the promised land. After Israel builds the golden calf at the foot of Mount Sinai, Moses goes out for forty days and forty nights and pleads with God to withhold his judgment. The rains of the flood last forty days and forty nights. Jesus is tested in the wilderness for forty days and forty nights where he focuses upon the will of his father.

The journey from Beersheba to Mount Horeb was nowhere near a forty-day journey. But Elijah needed forty days, to get his focus back again. And we'll see next time the dramatic way in which God consumates this forty-day period of testing for Elijah.

WOULDN'T IT BE NICE if the road to godliness, the road to being conformed to the image of Christ, was just a straight, level road with no pitfalls, no pit stops, no stretches in the wilderness? It would be nice, but that's just not the way the Christian walk happens. The fact is that the road to godliness, to maturity in Christ, is at times a painful road, in which over and over again we must experience the losing of our life, dying to self, surrendering our will, the coming to grips with the weakness of human strength and the strength of God working through us.

Some of you are with Elijah today — in the desert and under the broom tree. You are discouraged. It's no fun. And I am not going to try to make you feel bad or feel good about being discouraged. The issue is not how you feel about it. The issue is what you can do about it. And what you must do is once again recover your focus, get yourself focused once again upon . . . upon what?

Paul says in Colossians 3:2, "Set your minds on things above, not on earthly things. For you have died, and your life is now hidden with Christ in God." We set our minds on things above. We look to Jesus. We seek first the kingdom. We view life from the vantage point of our exalted position with Christ at the right hand of God.

These desert experiences are painful enough, even when they achieve their purpose — of leading us ever higher to the rock of our salvation. But the tragedy is when they are wasted, when we muddle our way through the desert and never gain from the low times in our life a renewed sense of vision, a new focus upon our life in the hidden depths of Christ.

Set your minds on things above, not on earthly things. See life from the perspective of the eternal. Catch the vision of the not yet. God rules. You are hidden with Christ in God. Mount Carmel, not the broomtree of Beersheeba, is the true picture of life in God's world. Believe it, and rejoice!

Kings 19:9-14

Proper 7
Pentecost 5
Ordinary Time 12

The Gentle Whisper

I can still remember the phone call that rainy Saturday evening. I had just arrived at my office from a day-long Council retreat, and was settling down to do some more work on my sermon for the next morning when the phone rang.

The voice on the other end told me to get to Flower Hospital immediately. Kim, the ten-year-old daughter of our best friends, had been hit by a car while she was running across Alexis Road, a busy five-lane city street. The only thing her older brother knew was that she was lying totally still on the road, and responded to nothing when they put her in the ambulance. And her hair was totally matted with blood.

For the next eight hours time stood still. First it was meeting Kim's parents in the emergency room. Then it was waiting for X-rays and a CAT Scan to come back and tell what was wrong. When those came back, it was waiting for an ambulance to transfer her to another hospital for more tests. Finally, late into the night now, it was sitting beside Kim's bed praying that she will wake up, looking at her, holding her hand, pacing the now darkened and quiet hallways of the hospital, praying, thinking, wondering.

At times like these our spirits are wide open to receive a revelation from the living God. At times like these we wrestle with realities like life, death, fear, hope, and love. All of our defenses are down. All the little details of our life that usually preoccupy us are erased from our soul. Nothing else matters now. We are suddenly open to even a gentle whisper from the living God.

This is the situation in which Elijah found himself in our text today. Elijah has been running for his life from Jezebel. God put him out into the barren wilderness for forty days and forty nights, preparing Elijah to receive a revelation from him. When Elijah finally arrives at Mount Horeb, God is ready to reveal something to Elijah.

God comes to him and says, "Elijah, what are you doing here?" And Elijah pours out his heart, "I've been such a good prophet for you, God. Everyone else has been so evil. I'm the only one left. And now they're trying to kill me too. Just look at me — this great prophet, stuck out here in the wilderness running for my life." A chorus of self-pity and self-defense!

God says to Elijah, "Go out on top of the mountain. I want to show you something. The Lord is about to pass by."

Elijah goes out, not knowing quite what to expect. First a tremendous wind comes up. It is so powerful that the mountains are literally torn apart. Rocks are flying everywhere. But God was not in the wind. And then there was a tremendous earthquake. The ground itself heaves. But God still is only preparing Elijah for the revelation of himself. And then comes a great fire. But God was not in the fire.

Now God has Elijah's total, undivided attention. Time stands still. Elijah's spirit is finally receptive to hear and to learn. And after the fire we are told that there came "a gentle whisper." God spoke. And Elijah was so terrified at having encountered, in this gentle whisper, *the living God* that he pulls his cloak around his face, and hastens back down the mountain to the mouth of the cave.

All of those days in the wilderness had been preparing Elijah to receive a revelation from God, to see the awesome power and glory of God that he was so much doubting when he had run for his life from Jezebel and had plunged himself into self-pity. And now God says to him, "I am the God of wind and earthquakes and fire. I rule this world, not Jezebel, not you. Trust in me!" And when he finally saw God for what *he* was, Elijah was overwhelmed with awe.

I do not believe that God ever sends us out into the wilderness just to leave us in despair. The wilderness is always a time of preparation, a time leading up to some new revelation from God. Whether that wilderness is a hospital waiting room, an unemployment line, the graveside, a broken relationship, a tear-stained pillow for whatever reason, God uses even these painful, broken times in our life to prepare the ears of our heart for a gentle whisper from him.

I have met many people in any number of the wildernesses of life, and am convicted that God never leads us through the wilderness without also beckoning us to go up on the mountaintop to receive a new revelation of God's glory and mercy. And if we will open our ears and hearts to him, we will hear this gentle whisper. And we will know God and ourselves in a new way.

Recently the Christian Reformed community of this city was shocked and grieved at the tragic news that a leader in our church community attempted, and almost succeeded, in taking her own life. I do not know Mary myself, but have learned that she has been in the wilderness for a long time. Disposed of by her husband, facing a divorce she absolutely refused to accept, much less condone, she has been out in the wilderness for over a year now.

I am sure that Mary knew, intellectually, that God doesn't lead us through the wilderness without calling us to the top of the mountain to a new and deeper understanding of his mercy and power. But that mountain just looked too far away from her recently when she swallowed a bunch of pills.

I repeat, God never leaves us in the wilderness (whatever your wilderness is today) without calling us to the mountain top to hear a new word from him. Our prayer for Mary is that this past experience will bring her closer to, and make her more ready to hear, the gentle whisper of God — that he loves her, that he cares for her, and that he will never let her go.

The wildernesses of life seem to drive us one way or the other. They either drive us deeper into ourselves, deeper into fear and loneliness and blame and self-pity, or they prepare us for a new and deeper grasp of the closeness and mercy of God. Wherever you are today, always keep heading toward the top of the mountain, from which you can look for God. Always be waiting for the gentle whisper of God.

I REALLY WISH that this story ended, "And Elijah was filled with a renewed trust and faith in God because he saw, before his very eyes, the awesome power and the gentle mercy of God. And he never feared Jezebel or felt sorry for himself again."

Unfortunately, that's not the way the story goes. The stories of our lives usually don't have such happy endings either. God now asks Elijah again, "What are you doing here, Elijah?" God wants to hear what Elijah's answer is, now that he has heard a new word from God. But he agains repeats, word for word, the same tale of self-pity and self-defense.

So what does God do now? Does God send him out again? No. He says, "Go!" He instructs him to *go* and anoint three different people; and he assures him that there are at least 7,000 other people who have not bowed the knee to Baal.

And the Lord said to him, "Go . . . " There comes a point in our dialogue with God when insight must be followed by *action*. Revelation by God is not enough. We must step out in faith and act upon that revelation. Elijah could have sat through a month of earthquakes and a chorus of gentle whispers, but the only way that those revelations would now become a part of his life would be if he got off his seat, stepped out in faith and *acted upon* what had been revealed to him.

That applies to us in the same way. The devil really isn't concerned that you are hearing the Word of God today. We pose no threat to Satan when we just sit and listen to the truth about God. The danger for the devil comes when we not only hear the Word of God but *act upon it*, let it transform our lives! A revelation from God that doesn't change us, that doesn't lead to some new action, to a transformation of our wills, to a new obedience is of no threat whatever to the prince of darkness. Sunday morning, when millions of Christians sit as spectators and listen to God's Word proclaimed, is not when the devil worries. Monday morning, this afternoon, five minutes after this service is when the devil shudders at the thought that people would not just *hear* God's Word, but would *go* . . . go out and act upon that word in a new way in their lives.

There's a saying that educators use that is so true. There are three parts to the saying: *(1) I hear . . . I forget.* Unfortunately, when we just hear a sermon or hear something else, we usually forget it quite quickly. *(2) I see . . . I remember.* If we don't just hear about a truth, but see it illustrated in some concrete way, we will at least remember it. That's why one professor of preaching I studied under a few years ago said, "You can preach the same sermon Sunday after Sunday, but you can never use the same story." We at least remember things we have seen with our physical eyes or with our mind's eye. "I hear . . . I forget. I see . . . I remember. *(3) I do . . . and I understand.*"

And the Lord said to him, "Go!" Step out! Do it! Do you dare to let the gentle whisper of God speaking to you *change* your feelings, *change* your attitudes, *transform* your priorities? Week after week, the gentle whisper of God comes to you and convicts you of something you have to do. To some of you, the gentle whisper says "You've got to deal with the problem in that relationship. Maybe it's a problem in your marriage or your family. Or the gentle whisper says, "You've got to face the fact that alcohol is ruining your life, and you've got to change." Or it says, "You've gone long enough pretending that just your example alone will lead your neighbor to Christ. You've had a dozen opportunities to share with her or him what Christ means to you. Now do it!" Or it says, "I have blessed you in abundance. It's time to return to God the tithe of money and talents and time that I have given you, starting today." Or it says, "Twenty years is long enough. It's time to forgive your father."

At different points in our lives, God speaks to us in his gentle whisper. If we will just go up to the mountain and listen with an open heart, we will hear him. The beauty of prayer is that it is a time to hear the gentle whisper of God. That's why we need a daily discipline of prayer, a time to hear God speak to us.

But as Elijah teaches us today, it's not enough just to hear God speak. We must act. We must go. If you go from this place and allow God to change just one thing in your life — notice I did not say, "allow God to convince you that you *should* change" — if you allow God to change one thing in your life that brings you one step closer to being like Jesus, the prince of darkness will shudder in horror. God will smile. And *you* will never be the same.

God has spoken. Go.

Kings 19:15-21

Proper 8
Pentecost 6
Ordinary Time 13

Our Higher Calling

How many of you are wearing the mantle of Elijah? God has just picked out Elisha to succeed Elijah as God's spokesman to the people of Israel. And Elijah places his mantle on Elisha to symbolize the calling that God has placed upon him.

God has placed that mantle upon each one of us today. If you do a study of the Old Testament, you will find that there were three specific offices, three spiritual vocations to which people were called and into which people were anointed — the offices of prophet, priest, and king. The prophets, priests and kings of Israel never just went into the personnel office of the temple and looked for a job. They were called by God, in a supernatural way, to be the person through whom God spoke and led the people of Israel.

When we study the New Testament, we find that Jesus Christ is the fulfillment of each of these offices. He is the chief prophet, the only high priest, and the eternal king. And if we look further in the New Testament, we see that now *all Christians,* all who share in the life of Christ, are prophets, priests and kings. We are all proclaimers of God's good news *(prophets).* We are all living sacrifices of thanksgiving *(priests).* We are all seated with the reigning Christ in the heavenly places at God's right hand *(kings).*

Again I ask, how many of you are wearing the mantle of Elijah? Put another way, how many of you are conscious of the calling God has given you to be the revelation of God himself? How many of you see God working through you to reveal his kingdom, to proclaim his love, to call people to trust in him?

That is what God calls Elisha (and us) to do and be in our text today. It's instructive for us to look closely at how Elisha responds to this calling. When we look closely at these verses, we see two different ways that Elisha responds to this call of God. And they represent two responses to the call of God that exist to this day.

Elisha's first response is in verse 20. Elijah has put his mantle on Elisha. Elisha realizes that he has now been called by God to be the prophet to Israel. And he now proceeds to make a rather innocent request of Elijah. He says, "I would like to go say good-bye to my father and my mother." Now, if Elijah had just said, "Fine, go ahead," this little interaction wouldn't be so significant. But Elijah's response is intriguing: "Go back again, for what have *I* done to you?" Elijah says, "Why are you asking *me* what you should do? What have I done to you? I'm not the one who called you. *God* has called you. You're not accountable to me. You're accountable to God."

Think how often we reduce the splendor of the divine call to the flimsy whim of other people's expectations! I observe a pattern in my own life and in the lives of others that is so predictable that I would almost call it a spiritual law. To put it in terms of myself, the law goes something like this: "The degree of concern I have about what other people think, and the degree to which I measure the validity of my walk with God by other's expectations is inversely related to how aware I am of my personal and total union with Christ.

When I am aware of my glorious position in Christ, aware that my life is not my own but is hidden with Christ in God, aware of the mantle of Christ's Spirit surrounding and controlling me, then the frame of reference for my thoughts, my feelings, my decisions, and my actions is Christ and Christ alone.

But when I am living with "me" over in this corner, and "Christ" compartmentalized over in this corner as "just my Savior," *but not as my life,* when I am not living with a total sense of my oneness with Christ, I am suddenly asking Elisha's questions. Suddenly other people's opinions and other people's expectations are important to me. I am no longer free, but have submitted myself once again to what Paul calls the yoke of slavery. Other people and forces and laws are controlling me instead of Christ and Christ alone.

Elijah says, "What have *I* done to you?"

THAT LEADS to the question, though, of how we can experience this pure call of God. How can I experience this union with

Christ in such a personal and powerful way that I have genuine spiritual freedom and poise to be God's spokesperson, to wear Elijah's mantle?

And that leads us to the next reaction of Elisha. In the New International Version's translation of verse 21, we read that Elisha goes to his father and mother, comes back, and proceeds to burn the plow and slaughter his oxen. Now what was Elisha doing here? He was totally destroying his means of livelihood. He was offering up, in a sacrifice to God, the symbols of a past way of life, and stepping out, in faith and commitment, into a totally new way of life. Elisha the farmer became Elisha the prophet. The closing words of our text are that "he set out and followed Elijah."

Now, you may be asking, "Does God want me to burn down my business? Does he want me to quit my job?" No, God doesn't want our business or our job. He wants much more than that. He wants us.

God can speak through us only when he and he alone possesses us. Christ can live through us, and proclaim the word of the kingdom through us, only when we have totally surrendered not just our plow and oxen but our very self to him. Jesus says in Mark 8, "If any man would come after me, let him deny *himself,* take up his cross and follow me. For whoever would save his life will lose it; and whoever loses his life for my sake and the gospel's will save it."

Do you want to wear the mantle of Elijah? Do you want your life to be a powerful statement for the kingdom of God? You must do nothing short of "lose your life." You must totally surrender your rights, your claims, your ambitions, your desires to Christ. You must burn the plow and slaughter the oxen.

I am thrilled to report this morning that at least one person in this congregation, during the course of this past week, decided to burn the plow and slaughter the oxen, to bid farewell to a past way of life, step out, and trust in the power of God. And I am happy that he gave me the freedom today to share his story.

A member of this congregation has been living in the hellish wilderness called alcoholism for many years. He finally came to the point this past week of acknowledging that he, in his own power, was helpless, and that he needed a power far greater than his own to overcome the ravages of this demonic disease. He admitted himself on Friday to a local medical center. But more importantly, he surrendered himself to the power of God.

There is not a more gruesome/beautiful, bitter/sweet picture than the picture of a person coming to the end of his own resources, falling helpless into the arms of God, and finding for the first time, in the moment of total weakness, the power of God.

It takes no courage, no courage at all, to go through life slugging it out in our own power, keeping up the charade that we and our attempts at fullness are anything but a total failure (Paul calls it "refuse") without Christ.

It takes courage to surrender all, to burn the plow and slaughter the oxen, to lose our life that we may find it, to die that we may live.

Paul says, "When I am weak, then I am strong." The person I've described to you could write a book on that verse today. Paul says that God's power is made perfect in weakness. God can finally use us and speak through us when we burn the plow and slaughter the oxen, when we tear down every obstacle of self that stands in the way of Christ living his life through us.

Do you want to wear the mantle of Elijah? Elijah says to you today, "Don't look to me. Don't look to others. Look to Jesus, the author and perfecter of your faith. And don't just look to him. Lose yourself in him. Burn the plow and slaughter the oxen!"

Make the song of your heart:

All to Jesus I surrender, all to him I freely give;
I will ever love and trust him, in his presence daily live.

All to Jesus, I surrender, humbly at his feet I bow
Worldly pleasure all forsaken, take me, Jesus, take me now.

All to Jesus I surrender, Lord, I give myself to Thee;
Fill me with Thy love and power, let thy blessing fall on me.

1 Kings 21:1-3, 17-21   *Proper 9*
Pentecost 7
Ordinary Time 14

The Interrupter

What a sad tale of human failure we have today in the encounter of Ahab and Naboth. At first it looks as though Ahab just might be a pretty good guy after all. There's certainly nothing wrong with Ahab wanting to make a legitimate business deal for the vineyard of Naboth. It's close to the palace. It would be a convenient place for his vegetable garden. So Ahab talks to Naboth about some of his ideas, "I'm flexible. If you want to trade for some other land, we can work out a trade. Or if you want me to buy the land outright, I'll do that too."

But that's where the problems begin. For Naboth, sensitive to the fact that this is a part of the family inheritance, refuses even to talk with Ahab about parting with the land. The land is a part of the family, and it will remain that. "Sorry, Ahab, but no deal."

Ahab goes home "sullen and angry." (verse 4) He pouts. He goes into his bedroom and lies on his bed and sulks. He refuses to eat. Here's a grown man acting like a two-year-old. This is not the first time, of course, or the last, that the sin of covetousness has taken its toll on the human spirit. God did not add the tenth commandment to the law of Moses to make for a round number. He recognized that contentment — accepting what God in his wisdom has given us, and not focusing upon *what we don't have* — is a basic human virtue, and that covetousness will destroy our spirit.

Well, on the scene comes Jezebel. You can almost see the wheels turning in her head as Ahab, sniffling in his bed, explains to her that he wants a certain vineyard, but nasty Naboth won't deal with him on it. She says, "Ahab, Ahab, haven't you learned any of my tricks? Aren't you ever going to behave like a king? Get out your roto-tiller! Consider the property yours." And she then proceeds to have Naboth framed as a scoundrel who has cursed the king. And he is stoned outside the city gates.

Now we might conclude that Ahab is an innocent party in Jezebel's action here. Jezebel didn't tell Ahab what she was going to do. From the text, at least, Ahab seems to be the last person to find out that Naboth is dead. But his reaction to that news shows what kind of person Ahab was as well. When Ahab finds out what has happened to Naboth (verse 16), he doesn't say, "Jezebel, why did you *do* that? I didn't want the property bad enough for you to kill someone for it!" No, he casually gets up, goes over to his latest acquisition, and begins staking out his garden.

As stories go, this story could easily end right here. And we could profitably spend the rest of our time today reflecting upon the disastrous effects of covetousness and the virtue of contentment. But the story has only begun. For in verse 17-23, we meet the main character in this story: God! Through his prophet Elijah, God has the last word in this episode.

And his word is not very pretty. He condemns Ahab's complicity in the murder of another person for this property, and gives notice to Ahab, "in the same place where dogs licked up Naboth's blood, dogs will lick up your blood — yes, yours!" Dogs in that day were more like wolves than what we think of as dogs. They were dirty, wild, undomesticated, and flea-ridden nuisances. They roamed wild around the country-side. True, it doesn't make it much nicer to know that your blood will be licked up by a lovable cocker spaniel instead of a smelly half-wolf. But the point here is that God has in store for Ahab a most humiliating, degrading consequence for his unconscionable sin against another human being.

Throughout the history of Israel and throughout human history, God functions as the great interrupter. He interrupts the downward spiral of human evil. When sinful, fallen people would totally obliterate the moral contours of this universe — in this case, the contours of truth, of respect for property, and of respect for human life — God interrupts this downward spiral of evil and proclaims, through his judgment, his passion for truth and justice.

This is a hard story — especially for people who really want their God to be some kind of divine Santa Claus. As C. S. Lewis says, most people don't really want God to be a father, who at times must be firm and tough as he raises his children. Most people want God to be a grandfather who, with "senile benevolence," just wants everyone to have a good time, no matter what the price, no matter what must be overlooked.

But our God is not a divine Santa Claus. He is a God of perfect love. The foundation of that love is his unswerving devotion to truth and justice — to upholding and preserving the moral contours of this universe, and to interrupting, in his own timing and good pleasure, the course of human history as it deviates from those contours. And that nature of God has not changed since Ahab's time.

THANKFULLY, THOUGH, there is a difference between the way God interrupted Ahab's life and how Ahab received and responded to God's interruption on the one hand, and the way that God interrupts the lives of those who are in Christ and that they (we) receive and respond to God's interruptions.

Ahab was not just a sinner. He was dead in his sin. His heart was hardened against God. He had no desire for or experience of a clean heart and a new and right spirit. Even his meekness at the end of this episode, which did move God enough to delay his judgment, was obviously not true contrition and repentance, in which case God could have withheld his judgment altogether as he did before with the children of Israel.

If our hearts are hard and our spirits dead, then we experience God's interruptions in our lives as judgment and condemnation.

But when we have trusted in the blood of Christ and have experienced the forgiveness of our sins and the renewal of our spirits, when we understand God's desire that we be like Christ, then God's interruptions are not acts of condemnation and judgment. Paul says, "There is no condemnation for those who are in Christ Jesus." Then God's interruptions are a means of disciplining us, teaching us, perfecting us, correcting our course, setting us more firmly on the high road of holiness.

God loves us more than we will ever know. He loves us enough to strip away something that has become an idol and taken the place of Christ. God loves us enough to take away a job that has replaced him as our source of security. He loves us enough to throw our lives into chaos about the time we have concluded that we are doing a pretty good job of running our private little universe. He loves us enough to spare us of being successful, when he knows that we can't handle success and keep it in the right perspective.

At that point, he is not doing those things to be mean, or to punish us, but to complete one more step in the building program — the program of conforming us more and more to the image of his Son.

In Hebrews 12 we're told that this race we run toward fullness in Christ is difficult. It takes perserverance. Sin will easily entangle us. We will get sidetracked and take our eyes off Jesus, the author and perfecter of our faith. And the writer of Hebrews says that when that happens the Lord will rebuke us. But he tells us not to lose heart when that happens, "because the Lord disciplines those he loves. (verse 6) In verse 9 he says, "We have all had human fathers who disciplined us and we respected them for it. How much more should we submit to the Father of our spirits and live!" He goes on and says that God's discipline is even better than that of our earthly fathers. "Our fathers disciplined us for a little while as *they* thought best; but God disciplines us for our good." And why does he do that? *"That we may share in his holiness."* He adds, "No discipline seems pleasant at the time, but painful. Later on, however, it produces a harvest of righteousness and peace for those who have been trained by it."

I can certainly relate to the painful interruptions of God in my own life as well as to the delay that exists in recognizing their benefit. When I was in high school, I remember thinking that I was absolutely the ugliest kid around. I didn't just think it. I knew it. I have rarely seen anyone with acne as bad as mine was in high school. I just couldn't understand what God could have possibly had in mind in making me be so ugly, and making me feel so terrible about myself. But now I know. I talk to people with those feelings every week, and I can still feel just how they feel.

Midway through my high school career, I got into trouble with the law one Friday night. I was grounded and curfewed so severely by the authorities that I just fell out of social circulation. I lost all of my friends. For almost one entire school year I was totally alone in the world. It was the most painful year of my life. But I really learned that year what it meant that Jesus was my friend. I couldn't figure out why he wouldn't introduce me to one or two of his other friends, but I at least knew *he* was *my* friend.

With nothing else to do that year, I decided I might as well study. I came to like studying for the first time, which was good for the seven years of college and seminary that God had in store for me.

Toward the end of that year, I even got some friends. We threw ourselves headlong into the debate team. We were good debaters and found our place. God used those experiences of speech and debate to affirm some interests and abilities in research and speaking, and to plant the seeds of a future calling to the ministry.

The Lord disciplines those whom he loves. He interrupts our course when it is not leading us toward his greater plan for our life. We often cannot see it at the time, any more than our children understand some of the discipline we impose at the time. But James says that such trials produce a steadfastness in us, which, when they have had their full effect (notice, we have to let *them* have *their* full effect), make us perfect and complete, lacking in nothing.

God doesn't just want us to be forgiven and heaven-bound sinners. He wants us to be holy and blameless, perfect and complete, lacking in nothing.

WE CAN BE SURE that God wept that day in Jezreel, not only because Naboth had died, but because Ahab, crushed though he was at God's violent interruption of his life, still would not surrender his hardened spirit to God. God's deepest desire, for Ahab and for all of us, is that we would know him, that we walk totally in step with him, that we would find not just our salvation but our very life in Christ.

And God will continue to direct all the events of our lives and of human history to that end, till the day that the kingdom has come, and that we finally see that Christ is indeed all in all.

In that day we will see that God's interruptions were not the morbid, hostile spasms of an angry God. In fact, we will see that they were not even interruptions, but were neatly fitted pieces of the eternal, gracious program of God to remake us into all we were meant to be.

We are God's workmanship. God is making us into beautiful replicas of his Son. Let God do his work!

2 Kings 2:1, 6-14

Proper 10
Pentecost 8
Ordinary Time 15

Ascension Power

What a powerful ending we have today to the dramatic ministry of Elijah! From the heights of Mount Carmel to the depths of the broom tree, from the tender prayers for a widow's son to the fiery judgment against a wicked king and queen — wherever we have seen Elijah, we have seen drama and power. For wherever we have seen Elijah, we have seen God at work! We have seen his kingdom marching onward. And we have seen ourselves who, like Elijah, have encountered the living God.

The drama today is preceded by a very touching, human scene, a scene that has all of the qualities of the best of farewell scenes that we would ever see in a movie or read in a book. Elisha is hurting badly as he contemplates the inevitable — the loss of his spiritual father and friend Elijah.

Elijah tries to spare him any more grief. He tells Elisha, "Why don't we just say goodbye now? I have to go to Bethel to bid farewell to the prophets there. There's really no reason for you to come with me. Let's just get it over with and say goodbye now." But Elisha won't hear of it. It's like the airport scene when our loved one who is going back to a distant city says, "Just leave me off out front. There's no use to park your car and come all the way to the gate with me." But we say, "No, we want to be with you as long as we can. We want to watch the plane take off and keep watching until we can't see it any more."

When they arrive at Bethel, the prophets there display all of the sensitivity of a bull in a china closet. They say to Elisha, "Did you know that Elijah is going to leave us today?" Elisha, already hurting badly because of this prospect, retorts, "I don't want to talk about it!" The same thing happens all over again in Jericho.

From Jericho they go to the last place they will ever be together on earth — to the bank of the Jordan. As they approach the river, Elijah takes off his cloak, rolls it up and strikes the water with it. And the waters miraculously divide! The two of them walk across, leaving the fifty prophets who were still with them on the other side.

It's just the two of them now. They look at each other, and Elijah says, "Is there anything I can do for you yet, Elisha?" And Elisha, probably struggling to contain his emotions, says, "Yes, there is, Elijah. Please let me inherit a double portion of your spirit." Elijah realizes that he was really talking about God's Spirit within him, and that God's Spirit was not his to give in any portion, let alone a double portion. So he says that if God allows Elisha to see his miraculous departure from earth, then Elisha will receive his request.

Those are their last words. Suddenly a chariot of fire and horses of fire sweep down and come right between Elijah and Elisha. And Elijah is swept up in a whirlwind. And Elisha cries out in worship and awe, "My father! My father! The chariots and horsemen of Israel."

WE HAVE MORE HERE than an exceptional ending to an exceptional man's life. This miraculous, fiery ascension of Elijah into heaven is a statement to the world of the ultimate power of God and the ultimate triumph of his kingdom. It was also a symbol, a sneak preview, a foretelling of the way that the chief prophet, Jesus Christ, would leave this earth when his work was complete. In Acts 1:9 we read that after Jesus gave his great commission, "He was taken up before their very eyes, and a cloud hid him from their sight."

And as if that is not attaching enough significance to Elijah's miraculous ascension, there is even more. This event is not only a promise of Christ's ascension; it is the shadow, the rumor, of *our* glorious ascension with Christ. In Ephesians 1, Paul recalls the power that God exerted in Christ when he raised Christ from the dead and seated him at his right hand in the heavenly places, far above all rule and authority, power and dominion, and every title that can be given. And he says that this power is now "in us who believe." But in Ephesians 2 he adds, "Not only is that power yours. God actually raised (past tense) *you* up with Christ and seated (past tense) *you* with Christ in the heavenly realms in Christ Jesus.

This verse raises the question of exactly what kind of relationship do we actually have with Christ? Is it just one of intellectual assent, of believing that there is such a person and that he did certain things for us and the world long ago? Or are we somehow mysteriously united with Christ? Paul says, "We died and our life is now hidden with Christ? And Paul says that this union with Christ extends even to our mysterious spiritual presence with Christ already *now* in the heavenly places.

I'd like to ask you to close your eyes for a minute and go with me. Everyone close your eyes and get into focus your picture of heaven. We all have some picture of heaven in our mind's eye. There at the center of everything is God in all of his majesty. And sitting at his side is Christ. And right next to Christ is another seat, and you are sitting on it — right beside Christ. As you slowly turn and look around, you see angels in every direction — thousands, maybe millions of angels. And they are all singing. You have never heard such a full, powerful sound. You join them in perfect harmony as you all sing praises to the Lamb and to the Father.

Now look down, straight down. You see the universe. And in the oceans of space that you thought were empty, you see layers and layers of spiritual forces — fighting it out with one another. Before this, you have never clearly seen Satan's invisible onslaughts, those hosts of spiritual darkness. Now you understand why, before you were exalted with Christ, you couldn't help but lie and hate and steal. But now you can see them clearly. Now you are above them. They cannot reach you. Satan cannot touch you.

Now look all the way down to earth. You see some familiar sights — people are running around in a frenzy. They're so tense. Some of them are arguing. They all seem to be afraid. They all seem to be looking for something. Most of them don't even know it, but they're looking for what you have — the peace and joy you have because you are one with the God of the universe.

Now open your eyes. Where are you? In heaven or on earth? That question will only sidetrack us. More to the point: from what vantage point do you live your life? from here or from heaven? Do you view yourself as one small force tossed about by a million other forces and pressures around you, in which you just struggle to keep your balance? Or do you see yourself as having a position in this universe with Christ which enables you to transcend those forces, to stand above and out of the reach of these forces?

Scripture says that we, in our union with Christ at God's right hand, are far above all rule and authority and power and dominion — any force that would seek to control us. Why, then, did you get so upset this week when your car ran out of gas? Why did a look of rejection by that person at work or school ruin your day? Why are you so anxious about a future that Christ totally and absolutely controls? Why do you feel so powerless over temptations when in fact you are out of Satan's reach?

We are not helpless, huddled Christians, nervously waiting for a better day! We have seen the chariots and horsemen of Israel! And they have lifted us to new heights, to a transcendent vantage point! Elijah blazed the path to the heavens that we have now taken when we said, "O Jesus, Lord and Savior, I give myself to thee." With that cry of faith and surrender, we climbed into the chariots and rode behind horses of fire!

It is true, though, that we do have an address "down here," though our permanent address is "up there." We do physically live "down here" even though we view life from the vantage point of "up there." And so the inevitable question arises, "Just how much of that ascension power of Elijah and Christ is ours *down here?* Elisha wondered about that very thing. Elisha wonders, "Now that Elijah is gone, what is left 'down here'? Has Elijah [or we may say Christ] not only ascended to heaven but also taken with him all of God's power and glory? Does God really enable us to live 'down here' not only from the perspective but from the power of 'up there'?"

Elisha concludes, "There is only one way to find out. Let's see if Elijah's cloak, his garment that divided the waters of the Jordan when he was here, will still divide the waters of the Jordan even though he is gone." So he strikes the water and asks, "Where now is the Lord, the God of Elijah?" "And the water divided to the right and to the left!"

Where is Christ? He's in heaven. But he is also here. And he divides the waters here where we live. Where are we? With Christ — above all things, but at the same time in the middle of all things. In the world but beyond the power of the world to hurt us. We are salt that influences the world but cannot be dissolved by it; light that shines in the darkness but cannot be overcome by it; saints who live so much beyond the grasp of this world that we can live in the middle of the world with poise and with love.

"Where now is the Lord, the God of Elijah? And the waters divided to the right and to the left!"

2 Kings 4:8-17

Proper 11
Pentecost 9
Ordinary Time 16

The Risk of Life

Several years ago a distraught wife came to me and unburdened her soul of something she had been carrying around for many years. Four years had passed since she had gotten entangled in an extramarital affair with someone at work. The affair absolutely devastated her. She broke it off in fairly short order and hoped the pain and guilt would just go away. When it didn't, she finally came in to see me, confessed her sin to God in my presence, and experienced for the first time his full forgiveness. It had affected her relationship with her husband to the point that she decided it was necessary to also confess this to her husband and seek his forgiveness.

The husband was devastated to learn of her unfaithfulness. I talked with him, and after several sessions together, he was still consumed with anger and hurt. I suggested to him that he now faced a choice. He could forgive his wife and trust her again, or he could continue to hang on to his anger and self-pity and the power he had to manipulate her by holding her sin over her head.

He gradually saw that there was nothing more she could do. She had confessed her sin. She had genuine remorse. She had recommitted herself to remaining faithful to her husband. Now he had to decide whether to take the risk of forgiveness and trust, or whether to grovel in his hurt and anger.

He chose the latter. The risk of *life* — new life for this relationship — was too great. He chose to stay in the pit of death.

God offers every one of us life, abundant life. The essence of this life is fellowship with Jesus Christ. It is so totally abiding in Christ (like a branch abiding in a vine) that it is really Christ who lives his life through us. But the life God offers us involves a step of total trust and obedience that few are willing to take.

In our text, God comes to the Shunammite woman and offers her life. He offers her life in the form of a child she had never been able to have. This child is a rich biblical symbol of the life God offers to all of us — in *his* Son, Jesus Christ.

But the intriguing thing about this passage is how the Shunammite woman responds to this offer of life. I'd like to suggest that her responses to Elisha (or to God) are typical responses of anyone who is faced with God's offer of life.

1. Resistance

Her first response (verse 16) is one of *resistance*. "Don't lie to me," she says. "I don't want anything to do with this. It has taken me years to accept the fact that I can't bear children, and the last thing I want to do now is open up this painful area of my life. As great as it would be to have a child, I don't want to take the risk of hoping and believing I will have a child now."

The life God offers involves a risk of faith. Jesus calls it losing our life, giving up our security, our control, our rights, our desires, our plans, and letting Christ call all the shots in our life. The man I told you about earlier weighed the benefits of a marriage relationship that would be alive if he would love and forgive with Christ's love against the risk of trusting his wife again, of having to be honest about his own needs and sins and fears. He turned down the offer of life for that relationship.

Unfortunately, this man is not the only person who faces such alternatives and resists God's offer of life. Some of you here today are absolutely miserable because you are so wrapped up in yourself. You are living a lie. You have masks that are so thick and so subtle that you're not even sure who you are. You are one thing on the outside, and something else on the inside. And you would love to be free. You would love it if you could have relationships that were really honest. You would love to quit playing all the games — relational games, professional games, social games, church games. God offers you life — a relationship with him in which you can lose yourself. The thought of being freed from this bondage to self looks appealing. But many of you have turned down the offer. The risk is too great.

There are other areas in which we resist God's offer of life. Some of you know very well what God has revealed in his word, namely, that the key to financial freedom and peace of mind lies in the act of giving. God's command to give back to him in proportion to his blessing to us is not just for his sake and his causes. God knows and makes clear to us that it's only when we take the step of faith involved in tithing back to him that we will gain the peace of mind that God will provide for all of our needs. Peace depends upon the act of giving. But too many look at that and say, "I'd rather be anxious and worried with *all* of my money than to give the full tithe to God and test his promise of peace and provision." God offers us life. But most never step out in faith to experience it.

No, this woman's resistance to Elisha's offer of life is not really hard to understand. We do it all the time. The abundant life is a life of faith. It involves putting our self totally on the line.

2. Resentment

Going on in the story, we find that the woman bears a son, but the boy becomes sick and dies. She immediately goes out to find Elisha, and when she finds him, she utters those famous words, "I told you so! I *told* you I didn't want to have my hopes raised and dashed again! I *told* you that I didn't even want to open that whole painful part of my life. Look at me now!"

Her first response to God's offer of life is *resistance*. But despite her hesitation, she stepped out in faith. But now, at this tragic turn of events, her response is one of *resentment* that things haven't gone the way she thought they should have.

How often haven't you stepped out in faith to God and discovered that things got a lot worst before they got better? You were in the middle of a crisis, and you stepped out in faith, trusting in God, thinking things would get better. Instead they got worse.

I recently worked with a person who is going through some severe problems in his marriage. In the course of our conversations, he confessed his sins and accepted Christ as his Savior and Lord. But things didn't get any better in his life. In fact, they got worse. His marriage appeared to be more in jeopardy than it ever was before. At that point he faced the choice of whether to let these circumstances destroy his fragile faith, let them be the evidence that God's promises aren't really reliable, and make him resentful of

God's seeming intrusion into his life; or to let these circumstances teach him how the Christian walk is more a walk of faith than he ever imagined.

This week I got together with two members of our church who are struggling with substance abuse. One of these two was sharing with us what led up to his totally putting his life and his problem in God's hands. He allowed me to share a part of our conversation with you this morning. He said, "Before I went in for treatment, I said to God, 'I want your will to be done in my life.' I thought I meant that. 'Whatever you want, God, do it.' But what I really meant, as I now look back, was, 'God, do whatever you want, but this is how I want you to do it. I don't want to have to go into a treatment center, or I don't want to have to do this or face that. Do your will, God, but this is how I what you to do it.' " What he discovered, and shared so beautifully the other night, was that God doesn't work the way we sometimes want him to. He shared how he had learned that the Christian walk is really a walk of total trust. It's saying, "God, lead the way, wherever that leads."

Deep down, we want to control our life. We want to trust in God, but we also want to keep to our game plan, our idea of how our life ought to play itself out. But when we live with that kind of divided faith we will be candidates for resentment and for constantly second-guessing the will and wisdom of God.

One of the painful discoveries that Job had to make was that *God is God,* and that he had to trust in God's wisdom and love not just when he could see God working in his life in a positive way. The plain fact is that we rarely learn this kind of trust any other way than in those trials of fire in our life in which we must clearly choose whether we're going to trust God *totally* or hold back.

This Shunammite woman is not in any mood to let go of how she feels life should go. She wants to get off this ride of faith right now!

3. Release

But God intervenes. With the power of God, Elisha raises the boy from the dead. He goes in the little lad's room, climbs up on the boy and actually lies on him — mouth to mouth, eyes to eyes, hands to hands. (verse 34) He gets up, paces the room, back and forth, and does it again. And all of a sudden, the boy begins to sneeze. And he opens his eyes.

Elisha has the Shunammite brought in. He says, "Take your son." And then we read in verse 37, *And she fell at his feet and bowed to the ground.* God has finally broken through! From *resistance* to *resentment* to *release.* Release from her fears, release from her doubts, release from her need to control, release of herself to the God of life. For the first time, she accepts God's gift of life and totally releases her life to God.

God offers every one of us life this morning. Abundant life. A life of freedom and joy and peace. But the reason there are so few takers is that the only way to experience that life is to totally release our life to Christ's.

From our human vantage point it's a risk. Hence the sermon title — "The Risk of Life." Of course, it's not really a risk, because God will always deliver upon whatever he promises. But in our own strength, by our own calculation, and from our small vantage point, it's too great a risk. The human instinct for survival and for protecting self is too great. We, by ourselves, will never take the risk of losing everything for Christ, of totally trusting in him. Only God's Spirit will move us to take that risk.

To borrow from the title of Scott Peck's popular book, this walk of total faith is certainly a "road less traveled." It is a door that is narrow, to use Jesus' words, and a door that few will enter. God's Spirit beckons you, "Choose life!"

Look at it this way. The most you can lose is your life. And then, Jesus says, you will finally have found life — in abundance.

Notes

Notes

Notes

Notes

Notes

Notes

Notes

Notes